"It's hard to connect with your child without first understanding where they are. As counselors and speakers at parenting events across the country, we spend a great deal of time teaching parents about development. To know *where* your child is—not just physically, but emotionally, socially, and spiritually, helps you to truly know and understand *who* your child is. And that understanding is the key to connecting. The Phase Guides give you the tools to do just that. Our wise friends Reggie and Kristen have put together an insightful, hopeful, practical, and literal year-by-year guide that will help you to understand and connect with your child at every age."

SISSY GOFF
M.ED., LPC-MHSP, DIRECTOR OF CHILD & ADOLESCENT COUNSELING AT DAYSTAR COUNSELING MINISTRIES IN NASHVILLE, TENNESSEE, SPEAKER AND AUTHOR OF ARE MY KIDS ON TRACK?

"These resources for parents are fantastically empowering, absolute in their simplicity, and completely doable in every way. The hard work that has gone into the Phase Project will echo through the next generation of children in powerful ways."

JENNIFER WALKER
RN BSN, AUTHOR AND FOUNDER OF MOMS ON CALL

"We all know where we want to end up in our parenting, but how to get there can seem like an unsolved mystery. Through the Phase Project series, Reggie Joiner and Kristen Ivy team up to help us out. The result is a resource that guides us through the different seasons of raising children, and provides a road map to parenting in such a way that we finish up with very few regrets."

SANDRA STANLEY
FOSTER CARE ADVOCATE, BLOGGER, WIFE TO ANDY STANLEY, MOTHER OF THREE

"Not only are the Phase Guides the most creative and well-thought-out guides to parenting I have ever encountered, these books are ESSENTIAL to my daily parenting. With a 13-year-old, 11-year-old, and 9-year-old at home, I am swimming in their wake of daily drama and delicacy. These books are a reminder to enjoy every second. Because it's just a phase."

CARLOS WHITTAKER
AUTHOR, SPEAKER, FATHER OF THREE

"As the founder of Minnie's Food Pantry, I see thousands of people each month with children who will benefit from the advice, guidance, and nuggets of information on how to celebrate and understand the phases of their child's life. Too often we feel like we're losing our mind when sweet little Johnny starts to change his behavior into a person we do not know. I can't wait to start implementing the principles of these books with my clients to remind them . . . it's just a phase."

CHERYL JACKSON
FOUNDER OF MINNIE'S FOOD PANTRY, AWARD-WINNING PHILANTHROPIST, AND GRANDMOTHER

"I began exploring this resource with my counselor hat on, thinking how valuable this will be for the many parents I spend time with in my office. I ended up taking my counselor hat off and putting on my parent hat. Then I kept thinking about friends who are teachers, coaches, youth pastors, and children's ministers, who would want this in their hands. What a valuable resource the Orange team has given us to better understand and care for the kids and adolescents we love. I look forward to sharing it broadly."

DAVID THOMAS
LMSW, DIRECTOR OF FAMILY COUNSELING, DAYSTAR COUNSELING MINISTRIES, SPEAKER AND AUTHOR OF ARE MY KIDS ON TRACK? *AND* WILD THINGS: THE ART OF NURTURING BOYS

"I have always wished someone would hand me a manual for parenting. Well, the Phase Guides are more than what I wished for. They guide, inspire, and challenge me as a parent—while giving me incredible insight into my children at each age and phase. Our family will be using these every year!"

COURTNEY DEFEO
AUTHOR OF IN THIS HOUSE, WE WILL GIGGLE, *MOTHER OF TWO*

"As I speak to high school students and their parents, I always wonder to myself: What would it have been like if they had better seen what was coming next? What if they had a guide that would tell them what to expect and how to be ready? What if they could anticipate what is predictable about the high school years before they actually hit? These Phase Guides give a parent that kind of preparation so they can have a plan when they need it most."

JOSH SHIPP
AUTHOR, TEEN EXPERT, AND YOUTH SPEAKER

"The Phase Guides are incredibly creative, well researched, and filled with inspirational actions for everyday life. Each age-specific guide is catalytic for equipping parents to lead and love their kids as they grow up. I'm blown away and deeply encouraged by the content and by its creators. I highly recommend Phase resources for all parents, teachers, and influencers of children. This is the stuff that challenges us and changes our world. Get them. Read them. And use them!"

DANIELLE STRICKLAND
OFFICER WITH THE SALVATION ARMY, AUTHOR, SPEAKER, MOTHER OF TWO

"It's true that parenting is one of life's greatest joys but it is not without its challenges. If we're honest, parenting can sometimes feel like trying to choreograph a dance to an ever-changing beat. It can be clumsy and riddled with well-meaning missteps. If parenting is a dance, this Parenting Guide is a skilled instructor refining your technique and helping you move gracefully to a steady beat. For those of us who love to plan ahead, this guide will help you anticipate what's to come so you can be poised and ready to embrace the moments you want to enjoy."

TINA NAIDOO
MSSW, LCSW EXECUTIVE DIRECTOR, THE POTTER'S HOUSE OF DALLAS, INC.

PARENTING YOUR FOUR-YEAR-OLD

A GUIDE TO MAKING THE MOST OF THE "WHY?" PHASE

KRISTEN IVY AND REGGIE JOINER

PARENTING YOUR FOUR-YEAR-OLD
A GUIDE TO MAKING THE MOST OF THE
"WHY?" PHASE

Published by Orange, a division of The reThink Group, Inc.,
5870 Charlotte Lane, Suite 300,
Cumming, GA 30040 U.S.A.

©2017 Kristen Ivy and Reggie Joiner
Authors: Kristen Ivy and Reggie Joiner
Lead Editor: Karen Wilson
Editing Team: Melanie Williams, Hannah Crosby, Sherry Surratt

Art Direction: Ryan Boon and Hannah Crosby
Book Design: FiveStone and Sharon van Rossum

Printed in the United States of America
First Edition 2017
1 2 3 4 5 6 7 8 9 10

Special thanks to:

Jim Burns, Ph.D for guidance and consultation on having conversations about sexual integrity

Jon Acuff for guidance and consultation on having conversations about technological responsibility

Jean Sumner, MD for guidance and consultation on having conversations about healthy habits

Every educator, counselor, community leader, and researcher who invested in the Phase Project

TABLE OF CONTENTS

HOW TO USE THIS ~~BOOK~~ ~~JOURNAL~~ GUIDE

The guide you hold in your hand doesn't have very many words, but it does have a lot of ideas. Some of these ideas come from thousands of hours of research. Others come from parents, educators, and volunteers who spend every day with kids the same age as yours. This guide won't tell you everything about your kid, but it will tell you a few things about kids at this age.

The best way to use this guide is to take what these pages tell you about preschoolers and combine it with what you know is true about your preschooler.

Let's sum it up:

THINGS ABOUT PRESCHOOLERS +
THOUGHTS ABOUT YOUR PRESCHOOLER =
YOUR GUIDE TO THE NEXT 52 WEEKS OF PARENTING

After each idea in this guide, there are pages with a few questions designed to prompt you to think about your kid, your family, and yourself as a parent. The only guarantee we give to parents who use this guide is this: You will mess up some things as a parent this year. Actually, that's a guarantee to every parent, regardless. But you, you picked up this book! You want to be a better parent. And that's what we hope this guide will do: help you parent your preschooler just a little better, simply because you paused to consider a few ideas that can help you make the most of this phase.

THE FOUR-YEAR-OLD PHASE

Who *really* knows what provokes that mischievous glint in the eye of a four-year-old just moments before they deliver the kick that makes the block tower tumble? I suspect it's something about the thrill of destruction combined with the wondrous spectacle of discovery.

Four-year-olds blend the reckless abandon of toddlerhood with the wide-eyed glimmer of preschool learning. You don't have to look very closely to see the wheels turning in that still-disproportionately-large head of theirs. They're taking in everything they possibly can about the big world around them, categorizing things, naming things, and putting it all together like a puzzle.

But the world of a preschooler is much more complex than the average puzzle. Every time your four-year-old learns something new, they will immediately discover three more things they never thought to ask before. Life is a maze of questions and answers that lead to more questions.

As a preschool leader at a church preschool, I still remember the day I was tasked with teaching the Ten Commandments. An especially advanced four-year-old child who could read our handout asked me what "adultery" meant. Caught off guard, I replied, "It has the word 'adult' in it, and when you are one, you'll understand."

Four-year-olds are notorious for asking questions that are hard to answer in four-year-old terms. Most parents of four-year-olds find themselves at one point or another stumbling through long, winding, well-intentioned explanations about things they aren't even sure they know how to answer in adult terms.

But don't overthink their curiosity. Most preschoolers will remember the reaction on your face and the tone of your voice far longer than they will the accuracy of your words. It's okay to leave some questions unanswered. Or, better yet, to only give the shortest, simplest answer possible. But just remember, the most extraordinary privilege is simply to connect to the heart of the four-year-old who is looking to you to guide them on their journey of discovery. We are, as exhausted explainers of every variety, quite beautifully, the first voice that gets to show the way.

Maybe that's what makes the four-year-old year the most incredible year for establishing a solid foundation in your preschooler's heart and mind. You are their first teacher. You are setting the tone for the elementary school years. So use this year to engage their wonder and imagination. Allow yourself a few minutes each week to get into their world and see through their eyes. Listen and learn alongside them. Let their curiosity remind you to ask a few questions about life that maybe you haven't considered in a very long time.

- JENNIFER WALKER
RN BSN, PEDIATRIC NURSE, MOTHER OF THREE, TODDLER CONSULTANT, AUTHOR AND CO-FOUNDER OF MOMSONCALL.COM

SECTION ONE

—

52 WEEKS

TO PARENT YOUR FOUR-YEAR-OLD

WHEN YOU SEE
HOW MUCH

Time

YOU HAVE LEFT

—

YOU TEND TO DO

More

WITH THE TIME
YOU HAVE NOW.

THERE ARE APPROXIMATELY

936 WEEKS

FROM THE TIME A BABY IS BORN UNTIL THEY GROW UP AND MOVE TO WHATEVER IS NEXT.

It may seem hard to believe, but at least 208 of those weeks have already passed you by. And, while things like giving your kid a cell phone, taking pictures before prom, or sending them off to college still feel far away, you're probably beginning to realize that your kid is growing up faster than you ever dreamed.

That's why every week counts. Of course, each week on its own might not feel significant. There may be weeks this year when all you feel like you accomplished was simply not falling to pieces when you saw just how many toys are now in your living room. That's okay.

Take a deep breath. You don't have to get everything done this week.

But what happens in your child's life week after week, year after year, adds up over time. So, it might be a good idea to put a number to your weeks.

MEASURE IT OUT.

Write down the number of weeks that have already passed since your preschooler was born. Then write down the number of weeks you have left before they graduate high school.

🔑 **HINT:** If you want a little help counting it out, you can download the free Parent Cue app on all mobile platforms.

_____

_____

_____

CREATE A VISUAL COUNTDOWN.

 Find a jar and fill it with one marble for every week you have remaining with your child. Then make a habit of removing one marble every week as a reminder to make the most of your time you have with your child.

Where can you place your visual countdown so you will see it frequently?

_____

_____

_____

_____

Which day of the week is best for you to remove a marble?

_____

_____

_____

Is there anything you want to do each week as you remove a marble? *(Examples: say a prayer, write in a baby book, retell one favorite memory from this past week)*

_____

_____

_____

_____

_____

_____

_____

_____

_____

_____

EVERY PHASE IS A

TIMEFRAME

IN A KID'S LIFE

WHEN YOU CAN

LEVERAGE

DISTINCTIVE

OPPORTUNITIES

TO INFLUENCE

THEIR

future.

YOU ONLY HAVE
52 WEEKS
WITH YOUR FOUR-YEAR-OLD

while they are still four.
Then they will be five,
and you will never know them as a four-year-old again.

That might be incredibly emotional,
or it might be the best news you've heard all day.

———————————————

Or to say it another way:
Before you know it, your preschooler will grow up a little more and . . .
learn to ride a bike.
tie their own shoe.
wash and rinse their own hair.

———————————————

Just remember, the phase you are in now has remarkable potential.
Before their fifth birthday, there are some distinctive opportunities
you don't want to miss. So, as you count down the next 52 weeks,
pay attention to what makes these weeks different from the rest of
the weeks you will have with your child as they grow.

What are some things you have noticed about your four-year-old in this phase that you really enjoy?

_____

_____

_____

_____

_____

_____

_____

_____

_____

_____

_____

_____

_____

_____

_____

_____

_____

_____

What is something new you are learning as a parent during this phase?

_____

_____

_____

_____

_____

_____

_____

_____

_____

_____

_____

_____

_____

_____

_____

_____

_____

_____

FOUR

—

THE PHASE WHEN
ANYTHING CAN BE
IMAGINED, EVERYTHING
CAN BE A GAME, AND ONE
CURIOUS PRESCHOOLER
WANTS TO KNOW,

"Why?"

IMAGINATION IS REALITY.

Your four-year-old's delightful imagination may suddenly turn your bedroom into a train station, a castle, or both. But imagination may also turn deceptive. Your four-year-old may suddenly insist the cat ate her cupcake, her bed somehow got wet from the rain, and maybe it was Grandma who spilled nail polish on the furniture.

EVERYTHING CAN BE A GAME.

You motivate your preschooler best when you appeal to their desire to play. Whatever the task, turn it into a game; make it fun. You might even let them take the lead and create a game you both can play. Your four-year-old is wired to have fun with you.

THEY HAVE A NEWFOUND CURIOSITY.

Whether it's showcased by pouring all the dish soap into the sink at once, or the constant repetition of "Why? Why? Why?", your preschooler is eager to know how the world works. So when they ask you "Why" for the second and third time, remember they're just looking for more of the knowledge they know you must have as an adult person.

YOUR

FOUR-

YEAR-

OLD

IS

changing.

PHYSICALLY

- Hops on one foot
- Strings beads and cuts with scissors (the plastic kind)
- Throws a ball overhand and catches a bounced ball (sometimes)
- Draws circles, squares, and a person with 2-4 body parts

VERBALLY

- Tells a short story
- Keeps a conversation going
- May struggle with some sounds: r, l, s, z, j, sh, ch, th
- Adjusts speech based on the listener and location

MENTALLY

- Sorts things and ideas into categories
- Recognizes less and more (especially if it's candy)
- Can argue, explain, and rationalize (you may have noticed)
- Lives in the present, but enjoys retelling the story of past events

EMOTIONALLY

- Tends to be optimistic in spite of failure
- Enjoys both physical humor and simple jokes
- Can learn relaxation techniques (take a deep breath)
- Often deals with fear and anxiety by distracting themselves

What are some changes you are noticing in your four-year-old?

_____

_____

_____

_____

_____

_____

_____

You may disagree with some of the characteristics we've shared about four-year-olds. That's because every four-year-old is unique. What makes your four-year-old different from four-year-olds in general?

_____

_____

_____

_____

_____

_____

_____

_____

What do you want to remember about this year with your four-year-old?

Mark this page. Throughout the year, write down a few simple things that you want to remember. If you want to be really thorough, there are about 52 blank lines. But some weeks, you may spend so many nights trying to get them back to sleep after a nightmare that you're too tired to write down a memory. That's okay.

_____

_____

_____

_____

_____

_____

_____

_____

_____

_____

_____

_____

_____

SECTION TWO

—

SIX THINGS

EVERY KID

NEEDS

YOUR KID NEEDS **6** THINGS OVER TIME

LOVE

WORDS

WORK

PEOPLE

STORIES

FUN

OVER THE NEXT 728 WEEKS, YOUR CHILD WILL NEED MANY THINGS.

Some of the things your kid needs will change from phase to phase, but there are six things that every kid needs at every phase. In fact, these things may be the most important things you give your kid—other than food. Kids need food.

EVERY KID, AT EVERY PHASE, NEEDS . . .

LOVE
to give them a
sense of WORTH.

STORIES
to give them a bigger
PERSPECTIVE.

WORK
to give them
PURPOSE.

FUN
to give them
CONNECTION.

PEOPLE
to give them
BELONGING.

WORDS
to give them
DIRECTION.

The next few pages are designed to help you think about how you can give these things to your four-year-old—before they turn five.

EVERY KID

NEEDS

love

OVER TIME

—

TO GIVE THEM

A SENSE OF

worth.

ONE QUESTION YOUR FOUR-YEAR-OLD IS ASKING

Life for your four-year-old can be confusing. It's okay to throw a ball, but not a rock. You can hug your friend, but not squeeze his neck. Your four-year-old is learning the rules for life and probably encountering some necessary discipline.

Your preschooler is asking one major question:

"AM I OKAY?"

Your preschooler needs to know you love them—even when they make bad choices. As the parent of a four-year-old, who may test your limits on a daily (or hourly) basis, you may feel overwhelmed at times. But remember this—in order to give your four-year-old the love and discipline they need, you need to do one thing:

EMBRACE their physical needs.

When you embrace your pre-schooler's needs, you . . .
communicate that they are safe,
establish that the world can be trusted,
and demonstrate that they are worth loving.

You are probably doing more than you realize to show your four-year-old how much you love them. Make a list of the ways you already show up consistently to embrace your preschooler's physical needs.

💬 You may need to look at this list on a bad day to remember what a great parent you are.

_____

_____

_____

_____

_____

_____

_____

_____

_____

_____

_____

_____

_____

_____

Showing love requires paying attention to what someone likes. What does your four-year-old seem to enjoy the most right now?

_____

_____

_____

_____

_____

_____

_____

_____

_____

_____

_____

_____

_____

_____

_____

_____

_____

It's impossible to love anyone with the relentless effort a four-year-old demands unless you have a little time for yourself. What can you do to refuel each week so you are able to give your preschooler the love they need?

_____

_____

_____

_____

_____

_____

_____

_____

_____

_____

_____

_____

_____

_____

_____

_____

_____

Who do you have around you supporting you this year?

_____

_____

_____

_____

_____

_____

_____

_____

_____

_____

_____

_____

_____

_____

_____

_____

_____

_____

_____

EVERY KID

NEEDS

stories

OVER TIME

—

TO GIVE THEM

A BIGGER

perspective.

BOOKS TO READ WITH YOUR FOUR-YEAR OLD

FEELINGS
by Aliki

THE HAT
by Jan Brett

STONE SOUP
by Marcia Brown

THE LITTLE HOUSE
by Virginia Lee Burton

STELLALUNA
by Janell Cannon

THE MONSTER AT THE END OF THIS BOOK
by Jon Stone

CORDUROY (SERIES)
by Don Freeman

PETE THE CAT (SERIES)
by Eric Litwin and James Dean

MAKE WAY FOR DUCKLINGS
by Robert McCloskey

THE LITTLE MOUSE, THE RED RIPE STRAWBERRY, AND THE BIG HUNGRY BEAR
by Don and Audrey Wood

STREGA NONA (SERIES)
by Tomie dePaola

ONCE UPON A MEMORY
by Nina Laden

THE STORY OF FERDINAND
by Munro Leaf

LITTLE CRITTER (SERIES)
by Mercer Mayer

CURIOUS GEORGE
by H.A. Rey and Margret Rey

THERE'S A WOCKET IN MY POCKET!
by Dr. Seuss

SYLVESTER AND THE MAGIC PEBBLE
by William Steig

THE EMPEROR'S NEW CLOTHES
by Hans Christian Andersen

GERALD AND PIGGY (SERIES)
by Mo Willems

A CHAIR FOR MY MOTHER
by Vera B. Williams

Kids need the kind of stories you will read to them over time. But they also need family stories. What can you do this year to capture your family's story so you can retell the story of this year to your child when they are older?

_____

_____

_____

_____

_____

_____

_____

_____

_____

_____

_____

_____

_____

_____

_____

_____

_____

What makes your family history unique? How can you preserve the story of your family's history for your child?

_____

_____

_____

_____

_____

_____

_____

_____

_____

_____

_____

_____

_____

_____

_____

_____

_____

_____

_____

_____

_____

Are there other stories that matter to you? What are they, and how will you share those stories with your preschooler?

_____

_____

_____

_____

_____

_____

_____

_____

_____

_____

_____

_____

_____

_____

_____

_____

_____

_____

_____

_____

_____

_____

_____

_____

_____

_____

_____

_____

_____

_____

_____

_____

_____

_____

_____

_____

_____

_____

_____

_____

_____

_____

_____

_____

EVERY KID

NEEDS

work

OVER TIME

—

TO GIVE

THEM

purpose.

WORK YOUR FOUR-YEAR-OLD CAN DO

DRESS THEMSELVES

WRITE THEIR FIRST NAME

MAKE SIMPLE SNACKS

SORT TOYS AND PUT THEM AWAY

SORT LAUNDRY
(darks / lights)

DUST LARGE SURFACES

HELP SET THE TABLE
(napkins and flatware)

PUT DISHES IN THE DISHWASHER

HELP PUT DETERGENT IN THE DISHWASHER

HANG UP WET TOWELS
(hang a hook on their level)

HELP CARRY GROCERIES
(the light ones)

What are some things your four-year-old has worked to accomplish so far?

_____

_____

_____

_____

_____

_____

_____

_____

_____

_____

_____

_____

_____

_____

_____

_____

_____

_____

_____

How are you giving your four-year-old opportunities to help out at home? What do you do to reward their efforts?

_____

_____

_____

_____

_____

_____

_____

_____

_____

_____

_____

_____

_____

_____

_____

_____

_____

_____

What are some things you hope your preschooler will be able to do independently in the next phase?

_____

_____

_____

_____

_____

_____

_____

_____

_____

_____

_____

_____

_____

_____

_____

_____

_____

_____

_____

_____

How are you helping them develop those skills now?

_____

_____

_____

_____

_____

_____

_____

_____

_____

_____

_____

_____

_____

_____

_____

_____

_____

_____

_____

_____

_____

EVERY KID

NEEDS

fun

OVER TIME

—

TO GIVE

THEM

connection.

WAYS TO HAVE FUN WITH YOUR FOUR-YEAR-OLD

GAMES:

CANDYLAND®

HUNGRY HUNGRY HIPPOS®

CHUTES AND LADDERS®

ANTS IN THE PANTS®

DON'T BREAK THE ICE®

COOTIE®

DON'T SPILL THE BEANS®

MEMORY®

ACTIVITIES:

PLAY-DOH®

ALPHABET LETTERS

FINGER PAINT, WATERCOLORS, OR PAINTBRUSH

SWING TOGETHER

CRAYONS

THROW OR KICK A BALL

24-PIECE PUZZLES

PLAY FREEZE GAMES

PLAY KITCHEN

PLAY "DUCK, DUCK, GOOSE"

PLAY "SIMON SAYS"

What are some activities that make you and your four-year-old laugh?

_____

_____

_____

_____

_____

_____

_____

_____

_____

_____

_____

_____

_____

_____

_____

_____

_____

_____

_____

_____

When are the best times of the day, or week, for you to set aside to have fun with your four-year-old?

What are some ways you want to celebrate the special days coming up this year?

5TH BIRTHDAY

HOLIDAYS

EVERY KID

NEEDS

people

OVER TIME

—

TO GIVE

THEM

belonging.

ADULTS WHO MIGHT INFLUENCE YOUR FOUR-YEAR-OLD

PARENTS

PARENT'S FRIENDS

GRANDPARENTS

NURSERY WORKERS

AUNTS AND UNCLES

BABYSITTERS OR NANNIES

List at least five adults who have influence in your
four-year-old's life right now.

HINT: They're probably the adults your four-year-old talks about.

_____

_____

_____

_____

_____

_____

_____

_____

_____

_____

_____

_____

_____

_____

_____

_____

_____

What is one way these adults could help you and your
preschooler this year?

EXAMPLES: pray for you, take your four-year-old to the library,
give advice to help you get ready for kindergarten

_____

_____

_____

_____

_____

_____

_____

_____

_____

_____

_____

_____

_____

_____

What are a few ways you could show these adults appreciation for the significant role they play in your child's life?

_____

_____

_____

_____

_____

_____

_____

_____

_____

_____

_____

_____

_____

_____

_____

_____

_____

_____

_____

EVERY KID

NEEDS

words

OVER TIME

—

TO GIVE

THEM

direction.

WORDS YOUR FOUR-YEAR-OLD NEEDS TO HEAR

The best way to begin preparing your three-year-old for school is by improving their vocabulary. Here are a few suggestions:

1.	2.	3.	4.	5.
Talk to your preschooler —the more, the better.	When they talk, make eye contact.	Give your preschooler opportunities to make choices.	Read, sing, or make up rhymes.	Join your child in pretend play.

What word (or words) describe your hopes for your child in this phase?

DETERMINED	MOTIVATED	GENTLE
ENCOURAGING	INTROSPECTIVE	PASSIONATE
SELF-ASSURED	ENTHUSIASTIC	PATIENT
ASSERTIVE	JOYFUL	FORGIVING
DARING	ENTERTAINING	CREATIVE
INSIGHTFUL	INDEPENDENT	WITTY
COMPASSIONATE	OBSERVANT	AMBITIOUS
AMIABLE	SENSITIVE	HELPFUL
EASY-GOING	ENDEARING	AUTHENTIC
DILIGENT	ADVENTUROUS	INVENTIVE
PROACTIVE	HONEST	DEVOTED
OPTIMISTIC	CURIOUS	GENUINE
FEARLESS	DEPENDABLE	ATTENTIVE
AFFECTIONATE	GENEROUS	HARMONIOUS
COURAGEOUS	COMMITTED	EMPATHETIC
CAUTIOUS	RESPONSIBLE	COURAGEOUS
DEVOTED	TRUSTWORTHY	FLEXIBLE
INQUISITIVE	THOUGHTFUL	CAREFUL
PATIENT	LOYAL	NURTURING
OPEN-MINDED	KIND	RELIABLE

Where can you place those words in your home so they will remind you what you want for your child this year?

_____

_____

_____

_____

_____

_____

_____

_____

_____

_____

_____

_____

_____

_____

_____

_____

_____

Don't be surprised if you find yourself wanting to text your four-year-old's comments to a friend—it's simply too good not to share. Just make sure to go back and write it down somewhere more permanent than your phone *(like here, on this page)*. The words of your four-year-old can become the stuff of great family stories for years to come.

SECTION THREE

—

FOUR CONVERSATIONS

TO HAVE IN THIS

PHASE

WHEN YOU KNOW
WHERE YOU WANT
TO GO,

AND YOU KNOW
WHERE YOU ARE
NOW,

YOU CAN ALWAYS
DO SOMETHING

TO MOVE IN A
BETTER DIRECTION.

OVER THE NEXT 728 WEEKS OF YOUR CHILD'S LIFE, SOME CONVERSATIONS MAY MATTER MORE THAN OTHERS.

WHAT YOU SAY, FOR EXAMPLE, REGARDING . . .

Pirates

Spiders

and Football

MIGHT HAVE LESS IMPACT ON THEIR FUTURE THAN WHAT YOU SAY REGARDING . . .

Health

Sex

Technology

or Faith.

The next pages are about the conversations that matter most. On the left page is a destination—what you might want to be true in your kid's life 728 weeks from now. On the right page is a goal for conversations with your four-year-old and a few suggestions about what you might want to say.

Healthy habits

—

LEARNING TO STRENGTHEN MY BODY THROUGH EXERCISE, NUTRITION, AND SELF-ADVOCACY

THIS YEAR YOU WILL

ESTABLISH BASIC NUTRITION

**SO YOUR CHILD WILL HAVE CONSISTENT CARE
AND EXPERIENCE A VARIETY OF FOOD.**

Maintain a good relationship with your pediatrician, and schedule
a well visit at least once per year. You can also begin to build
a foundation of healthy habits for your four-year-old with a few
simple words.

SAY THINGS LIKE . . .

DID YOU WASH YOUR HANDS?

LET'S PICK A HEALTHY SNACK.

THANK YOU FOR TRYING THAT.

WILL YOU THROW THE BALL WITH ME?

DID YOU KNOW CARROTS GROW UNDERGROUND?

I LOVE TO WATCH YOU RUN / RIDE / KICK THE BALL!

CAN YOU HELP ME COOK?

What can you do this year to help your four-year-old exercise? (Okay, "exercise" may be a stretch, but climbing and sliding and swinging count.)

_____

_____

_____

_____

_____

_____

_____

_____

_____

_____

_____

_____

_____

_____

_____

_____

_____

_____

What are some ways you might try to improve your
four-year-old's nutrition? Do they eat vegetables and
fruit regularly?

_____

_____

_____

_____

_____

_____

_____

_____

_____

_____

_____

_____

_____

_____

_____

_____

_____

Who will help you monitor and improve your four-year-old's health this year?

_____

_____

_____

_____

_____

_____

_____

_____

_____

_____

_____

_____

_____

_____

_____

_____

_____

_____

What are your own health goals for this year? How can you improve the habits in your own life—*you know, even though sometimes Saturday "lunch" consists of leftover Goldfish® crackers?*

_____

_____

_____

_____

_____

_____

_____

_____

_____

_____

_____

_____

_____

_____

_____

_____

_____

Sexual integrity

—

GUARDING MY
POTENTIAL FOR
INTIMACY THROUGH
APPROPRIATE
BOUNDARIES
AND MUTUAL
RESPECT

THIS YEAR YOU WILL

INTRODUCE THEM TO THEIR BODY

SO YOUR CHILD WILL DISCOVER THEIR BODY
AND DEFINE PRIVACY.

Your four-year-old may be so comfortable with their body they have no problem running outside in their birthday suit. That confidence is a good thing, but it's also a good time to start coaching them to understand privacy and personal boundaries.

SAY THINGS LIKE . . .

CLOSE THE DOOR WHEN YOU GO TO THE POTTY.

"IT'S POLITE TO LOOK AWAY WHEN SOMEONE IS CHANGING THEIR CLOTHES."

"CAN YOU GIVE YOUR SISTER SOME SPACE?"

YOUR FRIEND MIGHT NOT WANT YOU TO SIT ON HIS FACE.

"YOUR PENIS / VAGINA / BOTTOM / NIPPLES ARE PRIVATE, AND WE DON'T SHOW THEM TO PEOPLE."

"IF SOMEONE TOUCHES YOUR PRIVATE PARTS, COME AND TELL ME RIGHT AWAY."

"DON'T TOUCH YOUR PRIVATE PARTS IN PUBLIC."

"IT'S ALWAYS OKAY TO TELL SOMEONE 'NO' IF YOU DON'T WANT THEM TO TOUCH YOU."

"SOMETIMES THE DOCTOR MIGHT TOUCH A PRIVATE PART TO MAKE SURE YOU ARE HEALTHY. IT'S OKAY WHEN I'M WITH YOU."

When it comes to your child's sexuality, what do you hope is true for them 728 weeks from now?

_____

_____

_____

_____

_____

_____

_____

_____

_____

_____

_____

_____

_____

_____

_____

_____

_____

_____

_____

_____

Are you and your spouse, or your child's other parent, on the same page when it comes to talking about privacy? How might you work on a plan to communicate your hopes, expectations, and real-time conversations with your child?

_____

_____

_____

_____

_____

_____

_____

_____

_____

_____

_____

_____

_____

_____

_____

_____

_____

Write down a few things you want to communicate to your four-year-old about their body, right now in this phase. (They won't remember it all after one talk. It will take many talks, over time, to communicate what you want them to know.)

_____

_____

_____

_____

_____

_____

_____

_____

_____

_____

_____

_____

_____

_____

_____

_____

_____

Technological responsibility

—

LEVERAGING THE POTENTIAL OF ONLINE EXPERIENCES TO ENHANCE MY OFFLINE COMMUNITY AND SUCCESS

THIS YEAR YOU WILL

ENJOY THE ADVANTAGES

SO YOUR CHILD WILL EXPERIENCE BOUNDARIES AND HAVE POSITIVE EXPOSURE.

One advantage to technology is being able to play online games with your four-year-old. One disadvantage is that your four-year-old may not be a very magnanimous loser (if you happen to win). Either way, it's definitely a good idea to have some conversations about technology this year.

SAY THINGS LIKE . . .

LET ME SEE WHAT YOU DID.
(Show interest in what they do with technology.)

I'M TEXTING GRANDMA TO ASK A QUESTION.
(Talk openly about technology as you use it.)

I PUT MY PHONE AWAY WHEN WE ARE EATING SO WE CAN TALK TO EACH OTHER.
(Set limits for screen time.)

IT'S TIME FOR YOU TO PUT THE IPAD AWAY.

LET ME SHOW YOU WHAT A GALAXY LOOKS LIKE.
(Use technology to enhance your conversations.)

YOU NEED TO ASK BEFORE YOU USE THE COMPUTER.
(Know when they are on a device and what they are using it to do.)

When it comes to your child's engagement with technology, what do you hope is true for them 728 weeks from now?

_____

_____

_____

_____

_____

_____

_____

_____

_____

_____

_____

_____

_____

_____

_____

_____

_____

_____

_____

What rules do you have for digital devices in your family? If you don't have any, what are two or three that you might want to set for your four-year-old?

_____

_____

_____

_____

_____

_____

_____

_____

_____

_____

_____

_____

_____

_____

_____

_____

_____

_____

What are your own personal values and disciplines when it comes to leveraging technology? Are there ways you want to improve your own savvy, skill, or responsibility in this area?

_____

_____

_____

_____

_____

_____

_____

_____

_____

_____

_____

_____

_____

_____

_____

_____

_____

_____

_____

_____

_____

_____

_____

_____

_____

_____

_____

_____

_____

_____

_____

_____

_____

_____

_____

_____

_____

_____

_____

_____

_____

_____

Authentic faith

—

TRUSTING JESUS
IN A WAY THAT
TRANSFORMS HOW
I LOVE GOD,
MYSELF,
AND THE REST
OF THE WORLD

THIS YEAR YOU WILL
INCITE WONDER
**SO YOUR CHILD WILL KNOW GOD'S LOVE
AND MEET GOD'S FAMILY.**

Your four-year-old has many questions. Some might be about creation, heaven, church, and the Bible . . . and some of their questions might already be hard to answer. Don't panic. Just like other topics, answer faith questions as simply as possible. If they need to ask more, they will.

SAY THINGS LIKE . . .

> **GOD MADE YOU.
> GOD LOVES YOU.
> JESUS WANTS TO BE
> YOUR FRIEND FOREVER.**

> **WAS DANIEL AFRAID WHEN
> HE WAS THROWN INTO THE
> LION'S DEN?**
> (Talk about what your preschooler
> learns at church.)

> **"DO NOT BE AFRAID, FOR
> THE LORD YOUR GOD IS
> WITH YOU."** Joshua 1:9

> **ARE YOU SCARED?
> LET'S TALK TO GOD ABOUT IT.**

> **CAN YOU HELP ME CARRY
> THESE SOCKS?**
> (Prompt them to help.)

> **ISN'T THAT WONDERFUL?
> LET'S THANK GOD FOR IT.**

Who will help you develop your child's faith as they grow?

Is there a volunteer at your church who shows up consistently each week for your child? Do you attend a consistent service so your kid knows who will greet them each week?

_____

_____

_____

_____

_____

_____

_____

_____

_____

_____

_____

_____

_____

_____

_____

_____

_____

_____

_____

When it comes to your child's faith, what do you hope is true for them 728 weeks from now?

_____

_____

_____

_____

_____

_____

_____

_____

_____

_____

_____

_____

_____

_____

_____

_____

_____

_____

What routines or habits do you have in your own life that are stretching your faith?

_____

_____

_____

_____

_____

_____

_____

_____

_____

_____

_____

_____

_____

_____

_____

_____

_____

_____

_____

THE

rhythm

OF YOUR

WEEK

—

WILL SHAPE

THE VALUES

IN YOUR

home.

NOW THAT YOU HAVE FILLED THIS BOOK WITH DREAMS, IDEAS, AND GOALS, IT MAY SEEM AS IF YOU WILL NEVER HAVE TIME TO GET IT ALL DONE.

Actually, you have *728 weeks*.

And every week has potential.

The secret to making the most of this phase with your four-year-old is to take advantage of the time you already have. Create a rhythm to your weeks by leveraging these four times together.

Set the mood for the day.
Smile. Greet them with
words of love.

Reinforce simple ideas.
Talk to your preschooler and
play music as you go.

Be personal.
Spend one-on-one
time that communicates
love and affection.

Wind down together.
Provide comfort as the day
draws to a close.

What seem to be your four-year-old's best times of the day?

_____

_____

_____

_____

_____

_____

_____

_____

_____

_____

_____

_____

_____

_____

_____

_____

_____

_____

_____

_____

_____

_____

What are some of your favorite routines with your four-year-old?

_____

_____

_____

_____

_____

_____

_____

_____

_____

_____

_____

_____

_____

_____

_____

_____

_____

Write down any other thoughts or questions that you have about parenting your four-year-old.

YOU HAVE

APPROXIMATELY

728 WEEKS.

EVERY KID $\longrightarrow$ MADE IN THE IMAGE OF GOD

Incite *wonder* $\longrightarrow$ SO THEY WILL . . .
KNOW GOD'S LOVE
& MEET GOD'S FAMILY

BEGINNING
(Baby dedication)

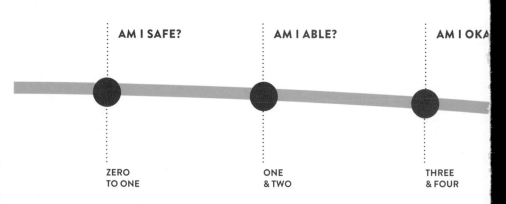

AM I SAFE?   AM I ABLE?   AM I OKA

ZERO
TO ONE

ONE
& TWO

THREE
& FOUR

EMBRACE *their physical needs*

TO **LOVE GOD**

Provoke
discovery

$\longrightarrow$

SO THEY WILL . . .
TRUST GOD'S CHARACTER
& EXPERIENCE GOD'S FAMILY

 WISDOM
(First day of school)

 FAITH
(Trust Jesus)

Y?

DO I HAVE YOUR ATTENTION?

DO I HAVE WHAT IT TAKES?

DO I HAVE FRIENDS?

K & FIRST

SECOND & THIRD

FOURTH & FIFTH

ENGAGE **their interests**

WITH ALL THEIR

 HEART   **SOUL**   **STRENGTH**

Provoke

→ SO THEY WILL . . .
OWN THEIR OWN FAITH
& VALUE A FAITH COMMUNITY

 IDENTITY
(Coming of age)

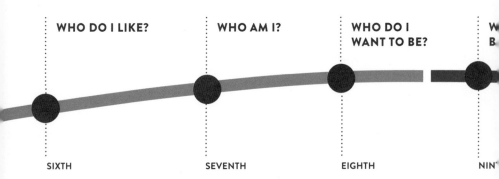

WHO DO I LIKE?   WHO AM I?   WHO DO I WANT TO BE?   W B

SIXTH   SEVENTH   EIGHTH   NIN

AFFIRM **their personal journey**

ND *trust Jesus* → TO HAVE A BETTER FUTURE

Fuel

passion →

SO THEY WILL . . .
KEEP PURSUING AUTHENTIC FAITH
& DISCOVER A PERSONAL MISSION

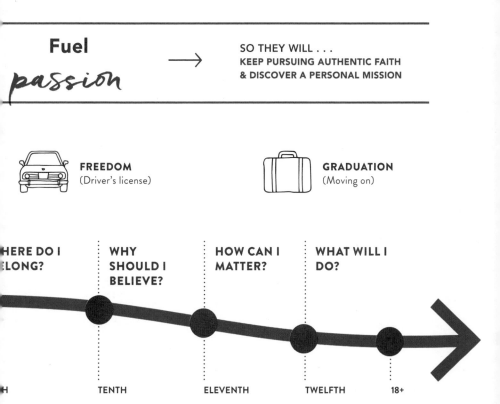

FREEDOM
(Driver's license)

GRADUATION
(Moving on)

HERE DO I :LONG?

WHY SHOULD I BELIEVE?

HOW CAN I MATTER?

WHAT WILL I DO?

H   TENTH   ELEVENTH   TWELFTH   18+

MOBILIZE their potential

IT'S JUST

A PHASE

SO DON'T

MISS IT.

_____

_____

_____

_____

_____

ABOUT THE AUTHORS

KRISTEN IVY @kristen_ivy

Kristen Ivy is executive director of the Phase Project. She and her husband, Matt, are in the preschool and elementary phases with three kids: Sawyer, Hensley, and Raleigh.

Kristen earned her Bachelors of Education from Baylor University in 2004 and received a Master of Divinity from Mercer University in 2009. She worked in the public school system as a high school biology and English teacher, where she learned firsthand the importance of influencing the next generation.

Kristen is also the President at Orange and has played an integral role in the development of the elementary, middle school, and high school curriculum and has shared her experiences at speaking events across the country. She is the co-author of *Playing for Keeps*, *Creating a Lead Small Culture*, *It's Just a Phase*, and *Don't Miss It*.

REGGIE JOINER @reggiejoiner

Reggie Joiner is founder and CEO of the reThink Group and co-founder of the Phase Project. He and his wife, Debbie, have reared four kids into adulthood. They now also have two grandchildren.

The reThink Group (also known as Orange) is a non-profit organization whose purpose is to influence those who influence the next generation. Orange provides resources and training for churches and organizations that create environments for parents, kids, and teenagers.

Before starting the reThink Group in 2006, Reggie was one of the founders of North Point Community Church. During his 11 years with Andy Stanley, Reggie was the executive director of family ministry, where he developed a new concept for relevant ministry to children, teenagers, and married adults. Reggie has authored and co-authored more than 10 books including: *Think Orange*, *Seven Practices of Effective Ministry*, *Parenting Beyond Your Capacity*, *Playing for Keeps*, *Lead Small*, *Creating a Lead Small Culture*, and his latest, *A New Kind of Leader* and *Don't Miss It*.

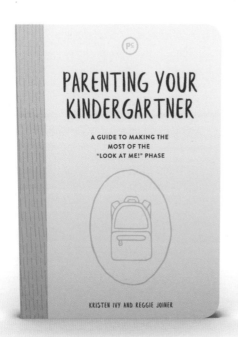

MAKE THE MOST OF EVERY PHASE IN YOUR CHILD'S LIFE

The guide in your hand is one of an eighteen-part series.

So, unless you've figured out a way to freeze time and keep your four-year-old from turning into a kindergartner, you might want to check out the next guide in this set.

Designed in partnership with Parent Cue, each guide will help you rediscover . . .

what's changing about your kid,
the 6 things your kid needs most,
and 4 conversations to have each year.

WANT TO GIFT A FRIEND WITH ALL 18 GUIDES
OR HAVE ALL THE GUIDES ON HAND FOR YOURSELF?

ORDER THE ENTIRE SERIES OF PHASE GUIDES TODAY.